Camping Cookbook

MW01268628

Fun, Quick & Easy Campfire and Grilling Recipes for the Whole Family

Direct & Indirect Grilling

Foil Packets

Open Fire Cooking

Louise Davidson

CONTENTS

INTRODUCTION

Camping can be a joyful experience, shared with friends and families alike. Being in the great outdoors brings people together, especially without the distractions of day-to-day affairs like work, cell phones, and the internet. Without these disturbances, families and friends can bond over hiking, swimming, games, and especially, food! The meal, the breaking of bread, is a time to come together and talk, to interact with each other in a way that our busy lives so often keep us from experiencing.

Family meals are important experiences to share. Magic can happen around the campfire when you're cooking and sharing great meals and stories together. Since none of these methods are regularly used at home, the many variations of camp cooking make the experience all the more unique. BBQ over a campfire, using coals, foil packet cooking, and more are all included in this cookbook!

Cooking techniques

Foil Packets

Cooking techniques while camping are unique. Aluminum foil packets are one of the most common methods included in the recipes. It consists of placing the food on an aluminum foil sheet and folding it tightly. The trick to foil packets is to keep the center seam at the top. This allows easy checking on the progress of the food, but also makes eating out of the pouch itself an easy possibility. They provide easy clean-up, with the fact that it is cook pot and serving dish all in one. Also, when cooking with foil packets you should not place the foil packets directly into the fire. Place them on a grill over the fire or on the coals once the fire dies down.

Open flames versus grilling

Certain recipes work well for cooking directly over the fire. S'Mores, foods that require boiling, and recipes that need charring do best over direct flame. However, most foods will cook best either on the grill (at a safe distance from direct flames) or on coals. Foil packets, for example, cook very well on hot coals. If you do cook directly on the grill, make sure the grill has been both cleaned and oiled.

Smokers and garbage can cooking

Another option for cooking is "garbage can cooking." This method requires a CLEAN metal can, and turns into a camping smoker. This works so well because it cooks foods very quickly at very high temperature. This keeps the juices in the meats and vegetables you are cooking and gives it a natural smoky taste that you can't get anywhere else. Large pieces of meat like turkey, pork roast, roast beef, and firm vegetables like potatoes are all great options when using this cooking technique. The complete method is detailed within the recipe and will certainly be the highlight of your trip. It is certainly has been for our family! It's also a great activity to do when feeding a large number of people since you can literally cook some 20-30 pounds of meat in a 20-gallon garbage can.

<u>Safety around the fire and cooking in the outdoors</u>

Much of the cooking within this book refers to open-flame style of cooking.
Fire safety is essential. Always keep an eye on the fire, never leave it unattended, and make sure that the fire is completely out, even if it is in a fire ring. Keep fire extinguishers at the ready, just in case.

Second, fire cooking is a tricky business. Until you know how to judge the heat of a fire or its coals, you may have some challenges first. The best way to attain success is to keep vigilant while cooking. Note that the best way to cook is directly on hot coals. This means you must have the time to start a fire, make it hot, and then let it die down into coals. If you do not have this time or patience, you might want to consider alternatives, as cooking over a flame though good, is trickier. Using a grill is helpful, and moving the food consistently may help prevent scorching. If you do not feel comfortable cooking over open flame, any camp stove will work quite well.

Do not forget to put the fire out after you are finished using it. One of the best ways to do this is to cover it with sand or dirt until it dies off completely.

Here are some additional tips regarding food safety. While this list is by no mean exhaustive, it is a good starting point.

- Washing your hands before and after handling food is an important safety rule to follow at all times. It may be even more so when cooking in the outside. You can also us hands sanitizers.

- Working on a clean surface, and keeping bugs and undesired creepy crawlers out of your food supply is also vital to avoid food poisoning. If you can, keeping your cooler in your car or trailer is a really good way to avoid contamination.
- Wash your fruits and vegetables with safe, drinkable water.
- Drink bottle you've bought or brought from home to make sure the water supply you use is safe to drink.
- Clean-up immediately after each meal, storing leftover food in airtight containers and away from night prowlers.

Food Security

All that said, special care should be taken when preparing your foods on site. Many of these recipes include foods that require refrigeration. Keep all foods in a cooler filled with ice or in a refrigerator until cooking. This is especially true for raw meats, dairy, and eggs. When preparing raw meats (and eggs), be careful not to cross-contaminate. This is when raw meat juices spread to other foods, like vegetables, which may be left raw. This is a problem because botulism and other bacteria can cause serious illness when consumed, even in small quantities. Make sure to wash hands, knives, and prep materials between each dish. Keeping a cutting board and knives for each food item (green for vegetables, white for meat, for example) can help prevent cross contamination. You may wish to prepare as much as possible prior to your camping trip.

Some essentials to bring on your trip:

For the fire
- ➤ Waterproof matches or a few good lighters
- ➤ Starter liquid fluid
- ➤ Starter wood
- ➤ Charcoals (plenty of it)
- ➤ Cooking utensils for barbecue: tongs, spatula, extra-long forks, cleaning brush for the grill.
- ➤ Grill (for over the fire, if the campsite does not provide or you like having your own)
- ➤ A grate to place directly on the fire to cook food on the open flame

To prepare and cook the food
- ➤ Large cast iron skillet or metal skillet that can be placed on the grill or fire
- ➤ Saucepan
- ➤ Heavy duty aluminum foil
- ➤ Cooking spray of your choice.
- ➤ Olive oil, butter

- Salt and pepper and other seasoning you may want to use, like garlic powder, chili powder, and other spices.
- Oven mitts (preferably silicone to accommodate very high temperatures)
- Can opener
- Bottle opener
- Prepping knifes, cutting board
- Whisk, spoons, wooden spoon, slotted spoon
- Grater, vegetable peeler
- Plastic strainer
- Large unbreakable serving plates
- Mixing bowl, various size
- Measuring cups and spoons
- Wood skewers
- Zip lock bags
- Mason jars – great for mixing dressings and has many other uses

To keep the food

- One cooler with plenty of ice or ice packs to keep perishable food and drinks fresh
- A second cooler or large plastic covered bin for dry non-perishable item like cans, pasta, rice, cereals, seasoning & spices.

- Plastic wrap
- Plastic airtight containers for food leftover storage

To Eat

- Non-breakable plates, glass, cups, mugs, utensils
- Napkins
- Plastic tablecloth
- Water bottles

To clean-up

- Paper towels
- Washing clothes, drying clothes
- Dish washing tub, dish washing soap

RECIPES

Each recipe has a specific requirement as far as cooking techniques and equipment are concerned. Make sure to read each recipe first before leaving on your trip to assure you have all necessities for the perfect camp meal. Having the basic essentials on-hand, just in case, is the best bet! It is also good to know that all the cooking times specified in the recipes are not set in stone and are our best approximation from our own experience cooking over campfires. They will depends largely on the heat that each barbecue and campfire produce. Please be vigilant when cooking your food. Checking it often is the way to go to avoid disappointment.

Enjoy the following recipes as a part of the magical experience of the outdoors. Make your trip memorable with photographs, unique activities, and delicious meals!

BREAKFAST RECIPES

Breakfast is the most important meal of the day! Start your camping excursion off right by making these delicious and hearty meals to energize your activities!

Big BBQ Breakfast Packets

One of the great joys of camping is what is commonly called "hobo meals." Combining foods into one "pot" or "packet" makes cooking and cleaning easier, but the resulting food combination is one you'll crave long after you're home. Here, your normal breakfast plate becomes a packet, cooked and eaten all together. You can make a really tasty burrito out of the completed packets!

Serves 4
Preparation time: 10 minutes
Cooking Time: 15-20 minutes

Cooking Techniques: foil packets
Equipment: 4 heavy duty foil aluminum sheets to make the packets

Ingredients

1 package of breakfast sausage (substitute: vegetarian sausage), thawed completely

2-3 cups leftover red potato wedges* (see Savory Sausage recipe)

6-8 eggs (lightly beaten, if you prefer scrambled eggs)

½ cup chopped tomatoes

1 small chopped onion

2 teaspoons salt

1 dash pepper

Cajun spice, if desired

4 tin foil packets

Spray oil

Hot sauce or ketchup (for topping)

Tortilla, if desired

Preparation method

Spray the foil with vegetable oil. Place 3-4 sausages on the bottom.

Place a few scoops of potatoes on top of sausages, followed by the vegetables. Crack one or two eggs or add already lightly beaten eggs on top of the mixture. Top mixture with seasoning and fold packets.

Allow to cook on a hot grill or coals for 15-20 minutes. When mostly cooked, open packets and add cheese. Return to heat and allow the cheese to melt.

To serve, eat directly out of the packet! Be careful as these will be hot! Top with ketchup or hot sauce. Serve with warmed tortillas.

If you don't have leftover potatoes, you can substitute grated fresh potatoes, store-bought fresh potatoes or breakfast hash browns.

Orange Sticky Buns

Sticky buns are a classic breakfast treat. The following recipe has a slight twist, though. Adding orange flavour as well as an orange hull makes these easy to clean up, eat, and certainly a unique experience!

\

Serves 4-6
Preparation time: 10 minutes
Cooking Time: 15 minutes

Cooking Techniques: foil packets placed on a grate directly on the coals, on the grill or a camping propane/gas barbecue
Equipment: 6 heavy duty foil aluminum sheets to make the packets

Ingredients
2 packages refrigerated biscuits
3 large oranges, halved and hulled (save the fruit flesh for side dish)
5 tablespoons butter
1/3 cup brown sugar
2 tablespoons maple syrup
2 tablespoons walnuts or pecans, chopped
1 teaspoon cinnamon (for topping)

2 tablespoons sugar (for topping)

Preparation method

Mix half the butter with all the brown sugar and maple syrup. Add to pan, and heat on the campfire grill until melted. Add nuts.

Drizzle some butter mixture evenly into the 6 orange hulls. Place 1-2 biscuit rounds in each hulled orange and top with some more butter mixture.

Cover orange halves with heavy tin foil, leaving enough place for the buns to rise. Place the oranges on a grate place directly on the coals. Cook for about 15 minutes, watching progress carefully*.
Remove from fire with tongs, and sprinkle sugar and cinnamon on top of each one.
Serve the orange flesh on the side or save for the Caramelized orange pork tenderloin dinner recipe.

*NOTE: You may have to place oranges above the coals/ fire on a baking sheet to allow them to rise as they bake.

Bistro Breakfast Panini

Try this unique version of this breakfast sandwich, balancing the savoury bacon and cheese with the sweet of the jam.

Serves 4
Preparation time: 15 minutes
Cooking Time: 3-4 minutes

Cooking Techniques: on the grill or a camping propane/gas barbecue
Equipment: a large cast iron skillet, 1 can cooking vegetable oil spray, 1 foil-covered brick (keep the foil clean!)

Ingredients
8 slices bacon (or pancetta. For vegetarians, there are bacon substitutes, or try thin slices of mushroom.)
4 bread-sized slices of a soft cheese like brie
8 slices thick bread (like sourdough or ciabatta)
Your favorite jam (suggested: raspberry, fig, plum)
Butter

Tip: Make extra bacon for the California Grilled Cheese Sandwich for lunch.

Preparation method

Cook bacon in the iron cat skillet over the grill, about 3-4 minutes on each side for a crispy bacon. Set aside on a plate covered with a paper towel. Roughly clean the skillet with a paper towel.

Butter the outsides of the bread. Spread the jam on one side, and then place the cheese on the other half. Add the bacon and put the sandwich together.

Place the sandwich, butter side down, on the pre-heated pan. Place the brick on top of the sandwich. Allow the bread to toast on one side, then flip sandwich over. Cook for 1-2 minutes per side until it's golden brown and the cheese has melted.

NOTE: The cook time refers to the sandwich only, and does not include the bacon.

Outdoorsy Oatmeal

An Oldie but Goodie, providing a variation of toppings, will make this heart-healthy and protein hearty meal a favorite with everyone!

Serves 4
Preparation time: 5 minutes
Cooking Time: 2 minutes

Cooking Techniques: on the grill or a camping propane/gas barbecue
Equipment: a large saucepan

Ingredients
Make-Ahead Mix:
2 cups instant steel cut oats
8 tbsp dried milk
4 teaspoons brown sugar
1 teaspoon salt
6 tablespoons of your favorite dry topping or mix

Combine the ingredients in a sealable bag for an easy, healthy, and quick-to-make breakfast.

Variation of toppings: raisins, chocolate chips, chopped nuts, dried bananas, dried apples, coconut flakes, dried fruits like apricots, chopped hazelnuts, cinnamon.

For Apple Pie Oatmeal: add ¼ cup raisins, dried apples, cinnamon, and chopped pecans.

Preparation method

In camp, place the Make-Ahead Mix in a saucepan. Boil some water over the fire or propane/gas camping stove. Add boiling water to your desired consistency (roughly 1.5 to 2 cups of water).

Stir and let sit for 2 minutes.

NOTE: *For non-dairy, leave out the dried milk. Boxed or canned coconut milk makes a great substitution after the oatmeal has been cooked.*

To serve, distribute oatmeal and allow each person to add their favorite toppings!

Campfire Skillet Breakfast

What better way to start the day then with a hot veggie and egg breakfast extravaganza! Excellent with grilled bread!

Serves 4
Preparation time: 10 minutes
Cooking Time: 35 minutes

Cooking Techniques: on the grill or a camping propane/gas barbecue
Equipment: a large skillet

Ingredients

3 tablespoon olive oil

1 medium onion, yellow

3 red peppers

1 zucchini

1 summer squash

3 large tomatoes, sliced

1 teaspoon smoked paprika

4-6 eggs

Salt and pepper, to taste

Preparation method

Heat oil in the skillet, adding the pepper and onion when hot. Cook about 8-10 minutes, until the onion begins to turn translucent.

Add the tomatoes and spices. Simmer for 15-20 minutes.

Clear a hole in the vegetables for each of the eggs. Add one egg to each well, and cook for 5 more minutes, or until the eggs are cooked to your liking. Season the eggs and vegetables with salt and pepper to taste.

Serve with grilled buttered bread.

Campfire Mexican Breakfast

One of Mexico's traditional breakfasts, "Huevos Rancheros," are delicious when prepared on the grill at your campsite!

Serves 4
Preparation time: 10 minutes
Cooking Time: 20 minutes

Cooking Techniques: on the grill or a camping propane/gas barbecue, foil packets, directly on the coals
Equipment: a large iron-cast skillet, heavy duty aluminum foil to make the packets

Ingredients

½ package bacon (can substitute vegetarian bacon or mushrooms)
½ onion, chopped
½ green bell pepper, chopped
1 jalapeno pepper, halved and thinly sliced
1 medium tomato, chopped
8 oz tomato sauce (or remaining enchilada sauce from Chicken BBQ Fajitas in Lunches)
8 large eggs
1 can refried beans

Warm corn tortillas

Preparation method

Heat the cast iron skillet directly on campfire or on the grill, roughly 4-5 minutes before cooking the bacon until it is golden and crisp. Remove bacon and d rain off all or most of the fat from the pan. Cook eggs "sunny side up." Remove eggs.

Add the onion, pepper, and jalapeno to the iron cast skillet. Cook until they begin to soften, about 2 minutes. Add tomato and sauce, and ½ cup water. Simmer. Heat tortillas in a large aluminum foil packet that you can place directly on the coals for 2-3 minutes.

For the refried beans, open the can and remove the label. Place it near the coals for a few minutes, until the beans are warmed through.

To serve, place one to two eggs on corn tortillas on each plate, topped by a few spoons of sauce. Serve bacon and beans on the side.

Tip: cook some extra bacon for the California Grilled Cheese recipe in Lunches.

BBQ Classic Breakfast Sandwich

How about an egg, Canadian bacon, and sharp cheddar cheese sandwich, the perfect breakfast, especially if the night was cold!

Serves 4
Preparation time: 15 minutes
Cooking Time: 10 minutes

Cooking Techniques: on the grill over the campfire or a camping propane/gas barbecue and/or foil packets
Equipment: a large non-stick skillet or iron cast skillet, camp "toaster" or heavy duty aluminum foil to make packets

Ingredients
6-8 slices Canadian bacon
½ onion, sliced
4-6 eggs
4-6 slices cheese, such as sharp cheddar
4 thick slices country-style bread
Butter
Stone ground mustard (optional)
Avocado

Preparation method

Butter your cooking pan and heat. Then, lightly grill the Canadian bacon on both sides, along with the onion. When the onion and the bacon have lightly browned, set them aside.

Cook eggs, in the style of your choice. Simultaneously, lightly toast the inside of the bread.

Spread butter on one half of the bread and mustard on the other. Add the bacon, then top with egg(s), onion, cheese, avocado slices, and the other slice of bread.

Place sandwich in camp toaster on the grill, flipping regularly. When cheese has melted, remove and eat!

NOTE: If you do not have a camp toaster, wrap in tin foil and place in the "coolest" part of the grill.

Power Pancakes

The classic of all breakfasts, this Make-Ahead Mix serves up a great deal of protein and fiber to keep you full, satisfied, and ready to conquer any outdoor activities.

Serves 4
Preparation time: 10 minutes
Cooking Time: 20 minutes

Cooking Techniques: on the grill or a camping propane/gas barbecue
Equipment: a large non-stick skillet or a large iron-cast skillet

Ingredients
2 large eggs
Vegetable oil
1 cup blueberries (if fresh is too difficult, substitute with ¼ cup dried blueberries)
Butter and maple syrup
2 cups of Make-Ahead Mix (recipe follows)
1¼ cup water

Make-Ahead Mix Ingredients:

2 ½ cups all-purpose flour

3 cups buckwheat (substitute: whole-wheat flour)

¼ cup flax seed, ground

¼ cup wheat germ

¼ cup packed light brown sugar

1 tablespoon baking powder

1 tablespoon salt (Kosher, preferably)

1 ½ tablespoon baking soda

1 ½ cups buttermilk powder

Mix all the ingredients in an airtight container or a sealable bag such as a zip lock.

Preparation method

Mix together 2 cups of the pancake mix with 1/¼ cups water, the eggs, and 2 tablespoons of oil. If you like, add blueberries and mix carefully. The batter should have some time to sit before cooking. In the meantime, heat a cast iron pan. Oil it a bit. When hot, start cooking!

Ladle roughly 1/3 cup portions into pan. Cook until edges are light brown with bubbles in the center. Flip once.

LUNCH RECIPES

When you're participating in camping activities requiring lots of energy like hiking and swimming, lunch is an important time to refuel! Try these recipes for a nutritious and easy meal to get you through the afternoon of outdoor adventure.

Couscous Salad

Not all meals need meat! This meatless, vegetable-filled lunch offers a variety of flavors, balancing the savory thyme with the sweetness of the couscous and the spice of the corn. And oh, yes, that corn! Use leftovers from the Mexican Corn on the Cob!

Serves 4
Preparation time: 35 minutes
Cooking Time: 15 minutes

Cooking techniques: grill over camp fire or camping propane/gas barbecue grill
Equipment: large iron-cast skillet

Ingredients
4 tablespoons olive oil
2 garlic cloves, sliced

3 cups dry couscous (preferably Israeli)

4.5 cups water

Fresh thyme sprigs

1 medium zucchini, diced

1 medium summer squash, diced

¼ cup pine nuts, toasted if possible

¼ cup corn (see Mexican Corn recipe)

Preparation method

Place the skillet over the grill, and heat the oil. Once heated, add the garlic and cook till soft, about 2 minutes.

NOTE: Be careful not to overcook the garlic! When garlic burns, it takes on a strong, almost acidic flavor.

Add couscous and vegetables, stirring. After about 5 minutes, the couscous should be toasted and lightly brown.

Add water and thyme, bringing the mixture to a simmer.

Allow to simmer until couscous is tender and water is absorbed. Remove from heat. Stir in pine nuts, adding salt and pepper to taste. Let the couscous salad sit for 5 minutes before serving.

Healthy Stuffed Baked Potatoes

This lunch recipe can also make a great dinner dish.

Serves 4

Preparation time: 5 minutes

Cooking Time: 45 minutes to 1 hour

Cooking techniques: foil packets and grilling over the campfire or camping propane/gas barbecue grill

Equipment: heavy duty aluminum foil to make the packets

Ingredients

4 large Idaho potatoes (or any other kind fit for baking)

Vegetable oil spray

Sea salt and pepper

1 small broccoli, washed, trimmed and cut into large pieces

Mozzarella cheese, shredded, for topping (or any of you favorite shredded cheese)

Bacon bits, for topping (optional)

Preparation method

Poke each potato with a fork. Slice each one in two and spread some butter on each side. Season each potato with salt and pepper if desired. Put the potatoes back together and wrap tightly with a double layer of aluminum foil. Place the potatoes directly on the campfire coals, you can even berry them under some of the coals. Let them bake for 45 minutes to an hour until they are fork tender.

In the meantime, spray lightly the broccoli pieces with vegetable oil. Cook directly on the grill over the campfire a few minutes on each side until just tender. Remove from heat and place on a plate. Cut the broccoli into small bite-size pieces and cover with foil to keep warm.

Note: you can also place an aluminum foil sheet on the grill to cook smaller broccoli pieces.

When the potatoes are cooked, open the foil packet, being careful about letting the steam out first. Mash each side of the potatoes with a fork, add some cheese and top with some broccoli and if you want, some bacon bits. Serve immediately.

Spatchcock Piri Piri Chicken

Spatchcock chicken refers to the flattening of the chicken itself, removing the backbone and cutting it so that it looks like a "butterfly." This reduces cook time, which is perfect for camping. Piri Piri refers to the spicy marinade that includes hot peppers and vinegar, which helps tenderize the chicken for faster cooking. It originates from Portugal.

Serves 4
Preparation time: 20 minutes
Marinade time: 1 hour
Cooking Time: 30 minutes

Cooking Techniques: on the grill or a camping propane/gas barbecue
Equipment: a brick wrapped with aluminum foil (or a flat rock if you can find one), a small mixing bowl and wooden spoon

Ingredients

1 whole chicken
4 red chilies, chopped
4 garlic cloves, diced
1 tablespoon sea salt

Pepper

1 teaspoon oregano

2 teaspoon smoked paprika

2 tablespoons red wine vinegar

2 tablespoons parsley, chopped

2 tablespoon olive oil

1 lemon, halved

Preparation method

Prepare your chicken before you bring it with you on your camping trip. It's a good idea to freeze it in and extra-large sealable plastic bag. Let it thaw only the day you will be cooking it.

To prepare your "spatchcock" chicken:

1. Cut wing tips and leg knuckles joints.

2. Remove the backbone.

4. Turn the chicken over, pressing down firmly until the chicken flattens out.

To prepare the Piri Piri seasoning, use a mixing bowl and a wooden spoon and blend chilies, garlic, salt, and pepper into a paste. Blend in olive oil, vinegar, and all spices. Mix well.

Rinse and pat dry the chicken with a paper towel. Rub the chicken skin with the lemon. Place the chicken in a shallow dish or a sealable bag such as a zip lock bag. Cover the chicken in the mixture. Allow it to marinate for at least an hour.

NOTE: You can marinate and then freeze the chicken raw ahead of time. By the time it defrosts at camp, it will be ready to BBQ!

Prepare your fire, making sure the coals are white hot when you start cooking the chicken. When it is ready, place the chicken (skin side down) on the center of the grill. Place a brick covered with aluminum paper on top. Allow to cook for 15-20 minutes until charred. Turn the chicken over, replace the brick on top and continue cooking for 10-15 minutes until the juices run clear.

Vegetable BBQ Pizza

Pizza takes on a whole new flavor when the dough is grilled over an open flame. Traditional recipes include pizza sauce, but you may want to shake it up and try BBQ sauce, especially if you have leftovers from the Savory Sausages recipe in Lunches.

Serves 6
Preparation time: 10 minutes
Cooking Time: 10 minutes

Cooking techniques: grill over camp fire or camping propane/gas barbecue grill
Equipment: baking sheet, large enough board to roll the pizza dough

Ingredients
Pre-made pizza dough (found at well-stocked grocers)
Garlic oil (1 clove in ¼ cup extra-virgin olive oil)
Mozzarella cheese, shredded
1 red tomato, sliced
¼ cup basil leaves
1 bell pepper, any color, trimmed and thinly sliced
½ white onion, thinly sliced
½ zucchini, thinly sliced
Jared A jar of pizza sauce or BBQ sauce

Preparation method

Drizzle the garlic olive oil over the sliced vegetables. Place the vegetable on a baking sheet. Grill briefly until they are just starting to be soft.

Roll pizza dough out using a pinch of flour. Brush the dough with the garlic olive oil and place on the grill, roughly 4-5 minutes (depending on thickness). Flip over with tongs once grill marks appear.
Immediately after you have flipped the dough, begin placing toppings on the pizza, finish with the shredded cheese. Cook until the cheese has melted and the dough has cooked, about 10-15 minutes. Make sure the grill is in the highest point position so the crust does not burn.

NOTE: If the fire is too hot, the dough will cook too quickly and the cheese will not melt appropriately, so watch carefully.

Chicken BBQ Fajitas, Enchilada Style

Using foil packets for campsite cooking makes cooking and clean-up easy, but it also makes delicious meals.

Serves 4
Preparation time: 20 minutes
Marinade Time: 30 minutes
Cooking Time: 30 minutes

Cooking techniques: Foil packets, placed directly on the white coals or on the grill over camp fire or camping propane/gas barbecue grill
Equipment: 4 heavy duty aluminum sheets, 1 sealable bag such as a zip lock

Ingredients
4 boneless chicken breasts, cut in thin strips ahead of time
1 Make-ahead Fajita Seasoning recipe (recipe follows)
1 large yellow onion
1 large green pepper
1 large red pepper
1 can enchilada sauce (optional)
1 package tortillas (12 small tortillas)
1 container sour cream or plain Greek yogurt

Shredded cheddar cheese or any Mexican cheese like
Cotija

1 small can sliced jalapenos

Make-Ahead Fajita Mix Ingredients

2 teaspoons chili powder

¼ teaspoon cayenne pepper

1 teaspoon salt

½ teaspoon cumin

¼ teaspoon garlic powder (not garlic salt)

1 teaspoon paprika

1 tablespoon cornstarch

1 teaspoon sugar

To prepare, mix all ingredients together in a small bowl. Pour into a sealable bag or airtight container for camping.

Preparation method

Marinate the sliced chicken breasts in fajita mix in a large sealable bag or shallow dish covered with plastic wrap. Make sure it is fully coated. Set aside for 15 minutes.

Slice peppers and onion in similar long slivers.

Place vegetables and chicken equally in the four heavy tin foil sheets. Add just enough enchilada sauce to lightly coat. Fold foil tightly, and add to grill or directly to coals.

Also, do NOT place packets directly into open flames, wait for the coals to become white. If you do not yet have hot coals, you can use the grill if that is an option.

Allow packets to fully cook, roughly about 20 minutes. Because fire temperatures vary, be vigilant and patient.

Warm tortillas either directly on the grill (but not over open flames), or wrapped in another sheet of heavy duty foil and placed on the coals.

To serve, remove from fire with tongs, and allow to cool for a few minutes. Open packets and add desired amounts to tortillas. Top each filled tortilla with sour cream or Greek yogurt, jalapenos, and cheese.

Grilled Greek Salad Pita with Beef Brisket

Serves 8

Preparation time: 15 minutes

Cooking Time: 6 minutes

Cooking techniques: grill over camp fire or camping propane/gas barbecue grill or foil packets

Equipment: 1 large heavy duty aluminum foil sheet, salad bowl

Ingredients

1 cucumber, peeled and cubed

1 pound left-over cooked beef brisket, sliced

1 tomato, diced

2 cups Romaine lettuce

8 halves of pita bread

½ cup feta cheese, crumbled

½ red onion, diced

Make-Ahead Dressing

2 ½ tablespoons chopped Kalamata olives

2 tablespoons olive oil

4 ½ teaspoon lemon juice

½ teaspoon dried oregano

1 healthy pinch black pepper

Preparation method

Make the dressing ahead of time and store in an airtight container like a small Mason jar or a plastic container.

Add tomatoes, cucumber, feta cheese, red onion, and artichoke to a mixing bowl. Add the dressing. Stir to coat well, and let stand for 5-10 minutes.

Over your campfire white hot coals, place the pita bread on the grill, or wrap in tin foil and place on coals. Heat for about 1 minute per side.

Fill each pita half with lettuce, beef, and vegetable mix.

California Grilled Cheese

Grilled cheese and the BLT meet…and are made even better.

Serves 4
Preparation time: 5 minutes
Cooking Time: 5 minutes

Cooking techniques: grill over camp fire or camping propane/gas barbecue grill
Equipment: iron cast skillet to cook the bacon if you don't have leftovers

Ingredients

8 thick country style bread slices
16 slices of bacon strips (leftovers from breakfast work fine!)
2 ripe avocados, sliced
8 slices cheese, like American or sharp cheddar
1 red tomato, thinly sliced
Butter
Parmesan cheese

Preparation method

If you have not saved bacon from one of the breakfasts, grill bacon until crisp on the grill in the cast iron skillet, and set aside.

Butter the slices of bread on one side. On unbuttered side of bread, add bacon, tomato and avocado slices, and cheese. Close with another slice of bread.

Place sandwich directly on the clean grill. On the side that's up, sprinkle parmesan cheese. Flip when bottom side is grilled nicely. Cook until cheese has melted, depending on the fire and grill placement, about 1 to 4 minutes per side.

Foil Packet Savory Sausages

What camping trip isn't complete without at least one hot dog meal? These meals are easily substituted for specific dietary needs as well. Choose your favorite spicy sausage, turkey hot dog, or vegetarian sausage option, and follow the recipe below!

Serves 4
Preparation time: 5 minutes
Cooking Time: 15 minutes

Cooking techniques: foil packets
Equipment: 4 heavy duty aluminum foil sheets to make the packets

Ingredients
4-6 sausages, your choice
5-10 red potatoes, sliced into wedges and pre-cooked (make extra and set aside for Big BBQ Breakfast Packets)
1 medium onion
1 summer squash
1 zucchini, sliced
Salt and pepper
Drizzle of olive oil

½ cup BBQ sauce

4 large heavy duty tin foil sheets

4-6 hot dog buns

Preparation method

Slice onion, summer squash, and zucchini to match size of red potatoes.

To prepare the packets, brush each aluminum sheet with olive oil or butter cooking spray. Add evenly split vegetables, and drizzle with a bit of olive oil, and season with a dash of salt and a pinch of pepper. Add 1 or 2 sausages, some precooked potato wedges, and a quarter of the BBQ sauce for each packet. Season with salt and pepper to taste. Fold each packet well. Allow packets to cook on coals or on grill over fire for about 10-15 minutes, depending on heat of coals or fire.

NOTE: Red potatoes can either be cooked ahead of time or baked on the coals in tin foil packets. Their cook time is much longer than the other vegetables, so you will want to cook them first.

To serve, place sausage in bun and top with vegetables. Add more BBQ sauce if needed.

Alternatively, it also tastes great without any bread, eaten directly from the packet.

Peppered Turkey Panini

Try this warm and toasty version of the turkey sandwich, balancing the savory turkey and cheese with the sweetness of the cranberries. What a great way to refuel!

Serves 4
Preparation time: 15 minutes
Cooking Time: 3-4 minutes

Cooking techniques: grill over camp fire or camping propane/gas barbecue grill
Equipment: iron-cast skillet, cooking spray, foil-covered brick

Ingredients

½ pound peppered turkey, thinly sliced
4 bread-sized slices Swiss cheese
8 slices thick bread (like sourdough or ciabatta)
Cranberry jelly
Lettuce leaves
Butter

Preparation method

Butter the outsides of the bread. Spread the cranberry jelly on one side and place the cheese on the other half. Add the turkey and lettuce and put the sandwich together.

Place the sandwich, butter side down, to the pre-heated skillet over the grill. Place the brick on top of the sandwich. Allow the bread to toast on one side, and then flip the sandwich over. Replace the brick. Cook for 3-4 minutes total, until golden brown and cheese is melted.

DINNER RECIPES

Garbage Can Dinner!

A few years ago, I went on a camping trip with some family friends. As we were planning our meals for the trip, we came across the famous "garbage can recipe" for turkey. We decided to try it out on our trip. Not only was it one of the best turkeys I have ever eaten, it was also the most memorable meal preparation of my life, and the highlight of our trip.

From then on, we experimented with different meats and even vegetables.

This recipe has three different proteins and potatoes. The way the meat and potatoes are placed while cooking makes all the juices from the meat drop onto the potatoes, giving them such a delicious flavor. The meats are barbecued and smoked at the same time, giving it an out of this world taste. It's a fantastic meal you'll want to have over and over again.
Invite the neighbors! You can definitely feed an army with this recipe.

Serves 15 + people with very healthy appetites!

Preparation time: 45-50 minutes   Marinade time: 30 minutes
Cooking Time: 3 hours

Cooking Techniques: garbage can cooking
Equipment:

- *a new 20 gallons capacity garbage can (galvanized metal). This garbage can will be used only to cooking. Don't use an old garbage can, this would not be sanitary.*
- *fireproof oven mitts/pot holders and silicone gloves/mitts that can handle very hot food*
- *1-2 large bag of charcoal – 4-5 pounds*
- *2-3 charcoal chimneys or 1 bottle of charcoal lighter fuel*
- *matches or lighter*
- *3/8-1/2 inch metal rod*
- *shovel and hammer*
- *latex gloves for the rub and barbecue sauce (optional)*
- *5 aluminum pans for the chicken, pork, beef and potatoes (2)*
- *plastic wrap*

Ingredients

1 chicken, 4-5 pounds

1 pork roast 6-8 pounds

1 standing rib roast beef 6-8 pounds

1 bag prewashed potatoes (10 pounds), washed

1-2 tablespoons BBQ seasoning for chicken

Kosher salt and pepper

1 bottle barbecue sauce

1 tablespoon paprika

2-3 tablespoons garlic powder

1 tablespoon prepared mustard

Preparation method

1. With your new garbage can, the first you need to do is fix the galvanization sealers the manufacturers coat the can with. For this, you will need to light up some charcoal. You can either use starting chimneys or charcoal lighter fuel. Light up the charcoal and let it burn until it becomes very hot. When the charcoal is starting to get hot, put some into the new garbage can with the shovel. Let it burn uncovered for about 20 minutes. Empty the can with thee fireproof oven mitts in a safe area, and keep the coals to use a bit later. Add some charcoal to burn so you are ready for later, about ¾ of the bag should be used.

2. In the meantime, prepare the meat. With clean hands or latex gloves, rub the chicken with the barbecue chicken seasoning and paprika. Make sure to clean your hands or gloves again before seasoning the pork and roast beef. You can also add some barbecue sauce if you so choose. Let the chicken rest in an aluminum pan and cover with plastic wrap. For the pork and the beef, season both generously with garlic powder. Mix mustard and butter and coat the roast beef. Rub the pork with some barbecue sauce. Put both roasts in an aluminum pan and cover with plastic wrap. Place chicken and meat in the cooler if you have the space.

3. Plant the rod with the help of the hammer where you are going to cook your meal. It should be a flat and clean area away from any flammable objects such as trees, tables, or chairs. The metal rod should be planted deep enough so that the garbage can fits properly over it, resting on the ground, so a little bit less than the can's height. Make sure the rod is clean as this is where the meat will be placed on. If it isn't, cover it tightly with aluminum foil.

4. Next, it's time to prepare the soil around your rod where the food will be cooked. Cover the ground around the metal stake with heavy duty aluminum foil strips,

enough to fit the garbage can over and about 1-1½ feet all around it where you are going to add the charcoal. Next, place a large aluminum pan through the metal rod and glide it to the bottom. This is where you will place the potatoes later.

5. It is now time to cook the food. Put the potatoes in the aluminum pan at the bottom of the rod. Then place the roast, beef bone first, on the rod and slide it down until it reaches the potatoes. Next add the pork, and finish with the chicken. Season the chicken, meat, and potatoes generously with salt and pepper. Place the garbage can over the meat and potatoes. If the can is still hot, use the fireproof oven mitts to place it.

6. With the shovel, add lots of hot charcoals all around the can and a bit on top so you have a row of coals there. Now it's time to relax and let the chicken, meat, and potatoes cook. It will take about 3 hours to get a medium-rare roast beef and perfectly cooked pork and chicken.

7. Monitor the charcoal around and on top of the can. Add some to maintain the heat. You might need to open a new bag depending on how fast your charcoal is burning. I always bring an extra bag in case.

8. After the 3 hours, it's time to remove the garbage can. To do this the first thing is to shovel all the remaining charcoal away from can and from the top. This way, you avoid getting some ashes touching your food. With the fireproof oven mitts/pot holders, delicately remove the garbage can. You should get some amazing aroma filling the air, and perfectly cooked chicken, meats and potatoes. Using silicone gloves, remove the food from the post and place in cleaned aluminum pans. Let the chicken, beef, and pork rest for 10 minutes before slicing and serve.

Note: If you want to reduce the amount of meat and potatoes of this recipe, just remember you can either reduce the cooking time accordingly or make it in a smaller garbage can and reduce the cooking time. Make sure the meat is not touching the inside of the can as it will stick and burn. A 20-25 pounds turkey will take 2 hours to cook.

You can watch several videos on the internet on this cooking technique. This is my favourite one from Sullivan Hardware & Gardens:
https://www.youtube.com/watch?v=SQP2OIH7zSc
This one from Cooking with Jack Show is also very good: https://www.youtube.com/watch?v=HIvrd68MjHQ

BBQ Chicken Pasta Salad

Have left over chicken from the BBQ Chicken and Mint-Tomato Salad? Use it here!

Serves 4
Preparation time: 5 minutes
Cooking Time: 10-12 minutes

Cooking techniques: grill over camp fire or camping propane/gas barbecue grill, foil packet
Equipment: large saucepan, strainer, large salad bowl

Ingredients

1½ cups cooked chicken breast leftovers or from a rotisserie chicken

3 cups dry penne pasta

1 tablespoon olive oil

1 tablespoon lemon

1 teaspoon lemon zest

1/3 cup parmesan cheese

1/3 cup feta cheese

¼ red onion, chopped

2 red tomatoes, diced

1 red bell pepper, cubed

½ tablespoon dry basil

1 clove garlic, finely minced

Salt and pepper to taste

Preparation method

Bring water to a boil in a large sauce pan using a camping stove or by boiling water over campfire. When boiling, add a generous amount of salt to the water. Add pasta and cook according to packaging instructions.

While pasta cooks, mix all the other ingredients in a large salad bowl, including the chicken.

Drain pasta with a strainer. Let pasta cool a little, and then add the pasta to the salad bowl. Mix well. Allow to rest for five minutes and serve.

Balsamic Beef Kebabs

Omitting the marinating time, this dish is a quick and easy meal to prepare, and is very tasty after a long day in the great outdoors.

Serves 4

Preparation time: 20 minutes

Marinade time: 2-8 hours

Cooking time: 12 minutes

Cooking techniques: grill over camp fire or camping propane/gas barbecue grill, foil packet

Equipment: 4-6 wooden skewers, soaked in water for 30 minutes, 1 large aluminum heavy duty foil sheet

Ingredients

2 pounds beef sirloin steak, cut in large and even chunks – 4-5 pieces per serving

4 cloves garlic, minced

2 teaspoons smoked paprika

1 teaspoon cumin

1 teaspoon Kosher salt

½ teaspoon black pepper

⅓ cup red balsamic vinegar

½ cup olive oil

4 white mushrooms, cleaned and trimmed

1 large onion cut large pieces

1 large green or red bell pepper, cut into large pieces

Garlic powder, to taste

Preparation method

In a large sealable plastic bag, mix oil, garlic, paprika, cumin, salt, pepper, and vinegar. If possible, use a mortar and pestle to mix ingredients into a paste. Add beef. Toss to coat well. Place the bag in the cooler and let marinate for at least 2 hours up to 8 hours. Turn the bag over at least once during marinating time

Spray some cooking oil or butter on the aluminum foil sheet, and add the onions, peppers and mushrooms. Season to taste with the garlic powder, and the salt and pepper. Make the packet by folding all sides. Cook on the grill about 2-3 minutes on each side. Let cool before opening the packet.

Place the beef cubes on skewers, alternating with onions and pepper pieces, finishing with a mushroom. Place on grill. Cook 2-3 minutes each side, until the meat is cooked to your preferred doneness. Remove from grill and allow to sit for 5 more minutes before serving.

Ginger and Lime Salmon

Fish is a staple camping dish, especially if you can catch your own. Give your dinner a bit of island flavor with this interesting combination of the spiciness of ginger and the tang of the lime!

Serves 4

Preparation time: 10 minutes

Marinade time: 30 minutes

Cooking Time: 15 minutes

Cooking techniques: grill over camp fire or camping propane/gas barbecue grill

Equipment: sealable plastic bag such as a zip lock bag, heavy duty aluminum foil

Ingredients

4 6-oz salmon (or tuna) steaks, skin on

1 fresh lime (sliced)

For marinade:

1½ tablespoons soy sauce

1 tablespoon olive oil

4 garlic cloves, crushed

2 teaspoons ginger, peeled and grated

1½ teaspoons sesame oil

¼ teaspoon red pepper flakes

½ teaspoon sugar

Preparation method

Place the fish inside a sealable bag, and add marinade ingredients. Mix well to coat the fish completely.

NOTE: Raw seafood should be handled with care. Make certain not to reuse anything that touches the raw fish without thoroughly cleaning it first.

Allow fish to marinate for 30 minutes. Occasionally turn the fish in the bag to make sure they are evenly coated. Remove fish from marinade. Save the rest of the marinade.

Place a sheet of heavy duty aluminum foil on the grill over the fire. Make sure the grill is set at the highest setting. Spray the sheet with cooking oil. Place fish, skin side down, on the foil sheet, then onto the grill, but not over a direct flame. Place thin lime slices over the top of the fish. Periodically baste with marinade.

Grill for 5-6 minutes per each ½ inch of the salmon's thickness. It should be done when the flesh flakes easily with a fork.

When ready, the fish should easily peel away from skin. Pair well with Baby Potatoes and Green Beans recipe (click for the recipes in the section Appetizers and Sides).

BBQ Chicken with Mint-Tomato Salad

This recipe is a lighter version of the traditional BBQ chicken. It comes with a refreshing accompaniment of a mint-tomato salad.

Serves 4

Preparation time: 40 minutes   Cooking Time: 10-12 minutes

Cooking techniques: Grill over camp fire or camping propane/gas barbecue grill
Equipment: sealable plastic bag such as a zip lock bag, salad bowl

Ingredients

4 boneless chicken breasts ⅔ cup olive oil

1 tablespoon lemon juice

1 teaspoon lemon zest

1 tablespoon honey

1-2 cloves garlic, minced

Salt and black pepper to taste

For the salad

¼ cup chopped fresh mint

⅛ cup chopped basil

1 pint cherry tomatoes, halved

Kosher salt to taste

¼ cup olive oil

Preparation method

In a bowl, mix together the salad ingredients. Stir a few times until all ingredients are well coated with the oil and salt. Set aside.

Mix olive oil, lemon juice and zest, honey and garlic in the sealable bag. Place chicken inside and coat. Let it stand for at least 30 minutes in the cooler, turning it over at least once.

Remove chicken from the marinade and place directly on the grill. Cook on each side, roughly 6-8 minutes, until the chicken breasts are cooked and juices run clear when pocked with a fork.

Remove chicken from grill, let rest for a few minutes. Serve with the tomato mint salad on the side.

Healthy Turkey Barbecue Burgers

A light and healthy burger option to the regular beef burger.

Serves 4

Preparation time: 10 minutes   Cooking Time: 20-25 minutes

Cooking techniques: grill over camp fire or camping propane/gas barbecue grill, cooking over open fire

Ingredients

1 eggplant

4 teaspoon olive oil

1 teaspoon lemon juice

1 garlic clove, minced

¾ teaspoon Kosher salt

½ teaspoon pepper

1 pound ground turkey

1 teaspoon soy sauce

4 burger buns, toasted over fire

Lettuce leaves and tomato slices to dress

¼ BBQ sauce and more for if desired

Preparation method

Slice eggplant and coat with olive oil, salt, and pepper. Place over grill, flipping a few times and cooking until soft.

Meanwhile, mix together oil, juice, garlic, salt, pepper, ground turkey, soy, and BBQ sauce.

Divide the ground turkey into four equal parts. With your hands, mash each section of turkey mixture into a patty. Place on pre-oiled grill, and cook on each side, roughly 3-5 minutes a side.

In the meantime, toast the buns on open fire. Make sure if you place them on the grill, it has not touched the raw turkey. Grill until just golden.

Place one slice of eggplant, lettuce, tomato on one side of toasted bun, and the cooked turkey burger on other side. Add more BBQ sauce if desired. Assemble and serve. Goes well with a side of coleslaw.

Grilled Rosemary-Garlic Shrimp Scampi Skewers

This skewer combination still carries the flavors of shrimp scampi but with an herby twist.

Serves 4

Preparation time: 10 minutes   Marinade time: 1 hour
         Cooking Time: 10 minutes

Cooking techniques: Grill over camp fire or camping propane/gas barbecue grill
Equipment: sealable plastic bag such as a zip lock bag, 4-6 wooden skewers, soaked with water for 30 minutes or more

Ingredients

1 teaspoon lemon juice

1 teaspoon olive oil

1/8 teaspoon salt

1 dash black pepper

2 garlic cloves, minced

2 rosemary sprigs

16-20 large shrimps, uncooked but peeled and deveined

Preparation method

Strip rosemary leaves off sprigs and chop them. To prepare the marinade, put rosemary, lemon juice, oil, salt, pepper, and garlic in a sealable bag. Add shrimp and coat well. Let marinate for an hour on ice.

Remove shrimp from marinade. Push skewer through shrimp in two places so the shrimp form a "c." (Hint: This keeps them from turning on the grill.) Place shrimp skewers on hot grill, turning after 3 minutes. Cook an additional 2–3 minutes just until done. Remove from heat, and place on serving platter. Sprinkle additional salt and pepper to taste if needed.

Classic Chili con Carne

What camping trip does not include a heartwarming chili con carne? This classic recipe can be prepared ahead of time at home and warmed up at the campsite or you can cook it completely on your trip. This recipe is for a campfire preparation.

Serves 4-6
Preparation time: 10 minutes
Cooking Time: 2 hours

Cooking technique: directly on camp fire on the coals and on the grill
Equipment: Dutch oven or large iron cast sauce pan with lid

Ingredients
1½-2 pounds lean ground beef
1 onion, diced
1 green bell pepper, trimmed and diced
2 cans low-sodium diced tomatoes
1cans red kidney beans
2 garlic cloves, minced
1-2 tablespoons vegetable oil

2-3 tablespoons make-ahead chili spice mix (recipe below)

Tex-Mex shredded cheese for topping

Preparation method

Heat 1-2 tablespoons oil in iron a large iron cast saucepan (or a Dutch oven) set on the grill over the campfire or on a camping propane/gas barbecue set on medium-high heat. Add the diced onions and garlic, and cook for 1-2 minutes until they are tender and fragrant. Add the ground beef and stir-fry until the meat is cooked through, about 5-10 minutes. Remove from heat.

Add diced green peppers, tomatoes and chili spices. Give it a few stir, cover with the lid and place directly on the white coals. Let is cook for 1 hour before adding the red kidney beans. Cook for an additional 30-45 minutes.

Serve in bowls and top with shredded cheese.

Make-ahead Chili Spice Mix

I usually make a big batch of this spice mix and keep in an airtight container. It's very versatile and can also be used as a rub to season meats and even for barbecue chicken and tacos!

Yields about 1 cup
Preparation time: 10 minutes

Ingredients

6 tablespoons chili powder

2 tablespoons ground cumin

2 tablespoons smoked paprika

1 tablespoon garlic powder

1 tablespoon onion powder

1 tablespoon dry oregano

1 tablespoon dry parsley

½-1 teaspoon cayenne pepper (add more or less depending on your heat level preference)

½-1 teaspoon crushed red pepper flakes (add more or less depending on your heat level preference)

1 teaspoon black pepper

½ tablespoon kosher salt

2 teaspoons packed brown sugar

Preparation method

Whisk all the ingredients together and place in an airtight container. It will keep up to 3 months at normal room temperature.

Caramelized Orange Pork Tenderloin

You can use the orange flesh from the Orange Sticky Buns in Breakfasts for this recipe!

Serves 4-6 (depending on the size of the tenderloins)
Preparation time: 10 minutes
Marinade time: 4 up to 8 hours
Cooking Time: 30-40 minutes

Cooking technique: Grill over camp fire or camping propane/gas barbecue grill (set on medium-high)
Equipment: sealable plastic bag such as a zip lock bag, large iron cast skillet, aluminum foil

Ingredients
½ cup orange marmalade
1 cup soya sauce
1/3 cup mustard, preferably stone ground
1 orange, juiced (take the pulp from sticky buns and mash through strainer)
½ tablespoon chili sauce
¼ cup brown sugar
1 tablespoon rice wine vinegar
2 garlic cloves, minced

2 pork tenderloins, about 1 to 1½ pound each, membrane and visible fat removed

1 onion

2 tablespoons olive oil

Preparation method

To prepare the marinade, put the orange marmalade, soya sauce, mustard, orange juice, chilli sauce, brown sugar, rice vinegar and garlic in an extra-large sealable bag. Add the pork to the bag. Make sure the meat is well covered with the marinade. Let it stand in the cooler for at least 4 hours up to 8 hours before cooking. Turn the bag over a few times during the marinating process.

Heat 1 tablespoon oil in iron cast skillet set on the grill over the campfire or on a camping propane/gas barbecue set on medium-high heat. Add the onion, and cook for 1-2 minutes until they are tender and fragrant. Add the tenderloins to the grill. Cook about 4-6 minutes on each side or until the meat is well cooked through. The center should be pink.

Remove from grill and let rest for at least 10 minutes before serving, cover with an aluminum foil paper to remain warm.

Chargrilled Sirloin Steaks with Potato Zucchini Feta Mash

A quick an easy dinner to fill you up after a day of activities! Classic combination of meat and potatoes!

Serves 4

Preparation time: 10 minutes   Cooking Time: 25-30 minutes total

Cooking techniques: Grill over camp fire or camping propane/gas barbecue grill set on medium-high heat
Equipment: large saucepan to boil water and cook potatoes, strainer, a potato masher

Ingredients

4 yellow potatoes, quartered

3 zucchini, cubed

½ cup hot milk

½ package feta, crumbled

1 tablespoon garlic butter

3 tablespoons butter

4 -6 to 8 ounces Sirloin steaks, ¾ to 1 inch thick

1-2 teaspoons garlic powder

1-2 teaspoon steak spices

Salt and pepper to taste

Preparation method

Boil the potatoes in water for about 10 minutes. Add the zucchini and continue cooking for another 4-5 minutes, until both the potatoes and zucchini are tender when stuck with a fork. Drain water. Add both butters. Cover the pot and let the butter melt. Mash with a potato masher. Add hot milk and cheese, and continue mashing until smooth. Season the potato zucchini mash with salt and pepper to taste. Cover to keep the mash potatoes warm while the steaks are cooking.

Season the steak with garlic powder, steak spices, salt and pepper. Let stand for 5 minutes before grilling. Place the steak on the grill over the campfire or on a pre-heated camping barbecue gas grill on medium-high heat. Grill the steak for 5-6 minutes on each side for a medium-cooked steak of 1 inch more or less.

Serve steak with prepared mashed potato-zucchini-cheese.

APPETIZERS AND SIDES

Mexican-Style BBQ Corn on the Cob

Corn is so inexpensive and easy to cook, it should be
the staple of every camp trip! Make a little extra corn,
and use it later for other dishes!

Serves 4
Preparation time: 5 minutes
Cooking Time: 15-25

Cooking techniques: foil packets
Equipment: heavy duty aluminum foil, corn holders
(optional)

Ingredients
8 ears of corn, husks on
½ cup butter, melted
2 limes
1 tablespoon chili powder
1 teaspoon salt

Preparation method

Let your corn soak in cold water for at least 30 minutes before grilling. Drain well and shake to remove excess water.

Mix butter, cheese, and spices. Add the juice of 2 limes. Peel back the corn husks, and smear the corn generously with the butter mix. Reseal the corn, then wrap each ear in heavy duty tin foil.

Cook on the coals for about 15-25 minutes, checking for corn to be tender, but still crisp.

To serve, remove from fire with tongs and allow to cool before removing the husk and leftover silk. If you have corn holders, use them after removing the husks.

NOTE: Leftover corn can be used for several recipes, including the Couscous Salad recipe in Lunches.

Greek Vegetable Kebabs

An excellent and healthy side dish. You can even eat this as a snack!

Serves 6
Preparation time: 10 minutes
Cooking Time: 20 minutes

Cooking techniques: grill over camp fire or camping propane/gas barbecue grill set on medium-high heat
Equipment: 6-8 wooden skewers, soaked in water for at least 30 minutes, mixing bowl, plastic wrap

Ingredients

8 oz. Halloumi cheese or any grilling cheese
1 yellow bell pepper
1 zucchini
6 cherry tomatoes
1 small bunch fresh mint
1 teaspoon dried oregano
3 tablespoons olive oil
2 tablespoons balsamic vinegar
Pepper and salt, to taste

Preparation method

Slice cheese into 1 inch cubes. Continue by cutting the bell pepper and zucchini into similar sized cubes. Dice the mint.

Toss cheese, vegetables, mint, oregano, balsamic vinegar, and olive oil together in a mixing bowl. Add salt and pepper to taste, and cover with plastic wrap. Let it rest for 15-20 minutes.

Evenly distribute all items onto each skewer, finishing with a cherry tomato. Place onto grill, and cook for 5-6 minutes before turning. Cook until cheese is golden brown.

To serve, use as a side dish, especially for the Couccous salad.

Spicy BBQ Baked Beans

What camping trip doesn't involve a good serving of baked beans! A good ol' Southern recipe, baked beans make a great side dish, especially to Savory Sausages recipe.

Serves 4
Preparation time: 15-20 minutes
Cooking Time: 2 hours

Cooking techniques: Grill over camp fire or camping propane/gas barbecue grill set on medium-high heat
Equipment: large-sized iron cast sauce pan – at least 2 quarts capacity

Ingredients

8 slices bacon, diced
1 medium white onion, diced
1 green bell pepper, diced
1 Granny Smith apple, peeled, cored, and diced
1-2 jalapenos peppers, seeds and membrane removed (more or less if you like spicy)
3 – 15 ounces cans navy beans
¾ cup BBQ sauce
½ cup brown sugar

¼ cup cider vinegar

1 teaspoon dry mustard

Preparation method

Begin by cooking bacon in the cast iron saucepan over the grill of the camp fire. Remove bacon and drain, keeping most of the bacon drippings in the pan.

Sauté vegetables in pan with bacon fat for about 5 minutes or until tender.
Add beans and all other remaining ingredients. Bring to a simmer.

Top the beans with the bacon, cover with the lid or with foil, and continue cooking until sauce has thickened. This might take up to 2 hours, depending on the fire.

Remove from heat, and allow to rest for 10 minutes before serving.

Baby Potato and Green Beans with Mozzarella "En Papilotte"

An easy to make and hearty side dish. It pairs well everything from grilled meats to poultry and fish dishes.

Serves 4-6
Preparation time: 10 minutes
Cooking Time: 25 minutes

Cooking techniques: foil packets, grill over camp fire or camping propane/gas barbecue grill set on medium-high heat
Equipment: heavy duty aluminum foil for packet making, mixing bowl

Ingredients

4 cups baby potatoes, washed and quartered

3 tablespoons pesto (jarred)

½ pound fresh green beans, washed and trimmed

Salt and pepper, to taste

8 oz. mozzarella, diced

Preparation method

In a large bowl, mix potatoes and green beans with pesto. Season the vegetables with salt and pepper to taste.

Make 4 aluminum foil packet sheets. Spray one side of each sheet with cooking oil spray. Place a quarter of the vegetables on each foil sheet and close to form the packets.

Place directly on the white coals, grilling for about 20 minutes or until potatoes are soft. Turn the packets over after 10 minutes.

Open foil packets and add cheese. Cook 2-3 minutes more without closing the packet and placing them on the grill to melt and lightly color the cheese.

To serve, this dish accompanies fish dishes like the Ginger and Lime Salmon perfectly.

Cocktail Sausage with Bacon and Maple Syrup

Nothing beats the salty deliciousness of sausage and bacon paired with the sweet delicacy of maple syrup!

Serves 6

Preparation time: 10 minutes

Cooking Time: 10 minutes

Cooking techniques: grill over camp fire or camping propane/gas barbecue grill set on medium-high heat

Equipment: saucepan, cast iron skillet, wooden toothpicks

Ingredients

1 cup ketchup chili sauce

1 cup maple syrup

24 oz cocktail sausage

1 pound bacon, each strip sliced in half

1 tablespoon vegetable oil

Preparation method

Place a saucepan on the grill and add the ketchup chili sauce and half the maple syrup. Mix together and simmer for 5 minutes, stirring and watching that it does not burn. Set aside.

Wrap each sausage with one half strip bacon. Secure with a toothpick cut in half (optional).

Add oil to cast iron pan. Place sausages seam side down on cast iron pan. Drizzle with remaining maple syrup and cook for 10-15 minutes, flipping until all sides of bacon have been cooked and are golden brown.

To serve, use sauce made earlier as a dipping sauce.

Indian Paneer Tikka

A delicious and flavorful Indian snack made over the fire.

Serves 4
Preparation time: 10 minutes
Cooking Time: 5 minutes

Cooking Techniques: Grill over camp fire or camping propane/gas barbecue grill (set on medium-high)
Equipment: sealable plastic bag such as a zip lock bag, heavy duty aluminum foil sheet

Ingredients
1 pound Paneer cheese
Cilantro or mint to serve

Make-Ahead Marinade
5 tablespoons plain yogurt
3 tablespoons tandoori masala
1 tablespoon lemon juice
2 cloves garlic, minced
1 small piece ginger, peeled and grated
Olive oil
Sea salt

Preparation method

Cut Paneer into even cubes.

Mix together all the marinade ingredients in a resealable bag like a zip lock. Put the Paneer into the marinade bag, and allow to rest for 1-2 hours in the cooler. Turn bag over a few times.

Place the Paneer cubes on an aluminum sheet, placed directly on the grill over the campfire hot coals for 4-5 minutes, turning periodically. Cook until lightly browned.

NOTE: Most well-stocked grocery stores will have the Indian spices. Otherwise, specialty stores should shelve them.

To serve, place on plate and sprinkle with herbs.

Easy Corn Bread Skillet

A delicious compliment to spicy dinners, this is a classic southern barbecue side dish that goes well with any barbecue dish.

Serves 6-8
Preparation time: 10 minutes
Cooking Time: 20-25 minutes

Cooking techniques: grill over camp fire or camping propane/gas barbecue grill set on medium-high heat
Equipment: large iron cast skillet

Ingredients

3 tablespoons butter

2 cups yellow cornmeal

1 teaspoon baking powder

½ teaspoon baking soda

½ teaspoon salt

1 large egg, lightly beaten

2 tablespoons honey

1½ cups buttermilk or whole milk

Preparation method

Put butter in cast iron pan. Place on the grill over the campfire until the butter melts. Remove from the fire with oven mitts and set aside.

Mix together all the rest of the ingredients in a large bowl. Whisk vigorously until the batter is smooth and lump free.

Pour batter into a hot cast iron skillet. Place it back on the grill of the campfire, cover and cook until golden brown and springy to touch, roughly 20-25 minutes. To make sure the cornbread is ready, insert a toothpick or a pointy knife, that comes out clean. If some wet batter is visible, continue cooking for a few minutes.

To serve, cut into slices and offer honey or butter to top the warm cornbread.

Teriyaki Chicken Skewers

The most time consuming part of this recipe is waiting for the chicken to absorb the teriyaki flavors of the marinade! This recipe yields a delicious appetizer before dinner!

Serves 6
Preparation time: 30 minutes
Marinade time: 60 minutes
Cooking Time: 30 minutes

Cooking techniques: grill over camp fire or camping propane/gas barbecue grill set on medium-high heat
Equipment: wooden skewers, soaked at least 30 minutes in water, heavy duty aluminum foil

Ingredients

1 10-oz. bottle Teriyaki sauce, preferably reduced sugar
¼ cup sesame oil
2 garlic cloves, minced
¼ cup lemon juice
1 tablespoon honey
2 pounds boneless and skinless chicken breasts, cut into half-inch strips

Preparation Method

Mix the ingredients for the marinade together in a sealable bag. Add chicken strips. Close the bag, and let sit for 1 hour in the cooler. Turn the bag over 2-3 times for a perfect coating of the chicken.

Place each chicken strip onto a skewer. Place the skewers on an aluminum foil sheet placed on the grill over the campfire hot coals. Watching carefully, allow to cook 6-8 minutes on each side, turning only once. If you want some grill marks, cook directly on the grill, but watch carefully as the sugary marinade has a tendency to burn easily.

Grilled Bread with Herb Butter

Garlic-herb bread is a great accompaniment to most of the dinners here, but it can also jazz up lunchtime sandwiches.

Preparation time: 15 minutes
Cooking Time: 5 minutes

Cooking techniques: grill over camp fire or camping propane/gas barbecue grill set on medium-high heat, direct fire cooking
Equipment: small saucepan, grilling forks

Ingredients
1 stick butter (½ cup)
2 garlic cloves, minced
½ cup fresh parsley, finely chopped
½ tablespoon dry chives (or 1 tablespoon of fresh minced chives)
1 loaf crusted country-style bread, sliced thick

Preparation method
Place butter in a small saucepan on the grill over the lowest heat. Keep away from the center of the fire. Add

garlic and chives. When melted, remove from heat and add parsley.

Brush one side of each bread slice with herbed butter. Grill butter side down over coals for about 2 minutes, until golden brown.

NOTE: You can make garlic herb butter at home before going camping. Place in the fridge until hard, and then in the cooler. Just melt the butter in the saucepan just before making toast. Also, consider making extra grilled bread for lunch sandwiches.

SWEETS

The best way to end the day? Enjoy some fire-roasted treats!

Some More, Some More!

An updated version of the all-time favorite S'mores!

Serves 4
Preparation time: 5 minutes
Cooking Time: 5

Cooking techniques: directly on the open flame
Equipment: long grilling forks or 4 long wooden sticks

Ingredients
1 package cinnamon graham crackers
2 blocks DARK chocolate, orange-flavored and chopped
1 package extra-large marshmallows

Preparation method
Place a piece of chocolate inside marshmallows. Skewer on your grilling fork or stick 1 or 2 marshmallows and carefully roast. When the marshmallow is puffed up and toasted, place between two cinnamon graham crackers.

To serve, merely eat...but carefully! This can be very hot and quite messy!

Apple Crisp Fritters

The following recipe is a mix between fritters and an apple crisp.

Serves 4
Preparation time: 10 minutes
Cooking Time: 5-10 minutes

Cooking techniques: grill over camp fire or camping propane/gas barbecue grill set on medium-high heat
Equipment: large iron cast skillet, mixing bowl

Ingredients
1 box instant biscuit mix

¼ cup instant steel cut oats

¾ cup whole milk

3 tbsp packed brown sugar

¼ cup granulated sugar

½ teaspoon ground cinnamon

⅛ teaspoon ground nutmeg

3 large green apples, peeled, cored and sliced

3 tablespoons butter

Preparation method

In a large mixing bowl, add sugar, brown sugar, nutmeg, and cinnamon. Stir well. Set aside 2 tablespoons of the spiced sugar for the topping. Add to the bowl the biscuit mix, oats, milk, and apples. Stir to coat the ingredients well.

Place the cast iron pan directly on the hot coals and add butter. Allow butter to melt in pan. With potholders, swirl the butter to cover the whole skillet well, making sure it's spread evenly. Add batter and cover (with tin foil if you have no lid). Place back on the coals and cook for roughly 5-10 minutes, depending if the fire is very hot. Let rest for 15 to 20 minutes before removing the cover.

To serve, sprinkle sugar-topping mixture over top as it cools. Slice, and serve.

Grilled Pineapple with Cinnamon Sugar

The tang of the pineapple with the sweetness of the sugar makes this healthy dessert a delicious treat.

Serves 4-6
Preparation time: 10 minutes
Cooking Time: 10

Cooking techniques: Grill over camp fire or camping propane/gas barbecue grill set on medium-high heat
Equipment: sealable bag such as a zip lock

Ingredients

1 cup brown sugar

2 teaspoons ground cinnamon

1 pineapple, cut, cored, sliced into 6 wedges

Preparation method

Mix sugar and cinnamon together and pour into a sealable bag. Add the pineapple wedges, seal the bag, and shake. Make certain each piece is coated well. Place the pineapple pieces directly on the grill. Cook for 3-5 minutes a side, until the sugar melts, and there are nice grilling marks on the pineapple.

Banana Chocolate Surprises

Easily a favorite in any campsite, this tasty treat has a new twist here.

Serves 4
Preparation time: 5 minutes
Cooking Time: 10-15 minutes

Cooking techniques: foil packets
Equipment: extra duty aluminum foil to wrap each banana

Ingredients

5 bananas, unpeeled
1¾ cup semi-sweet chocolate chips (mini M&M and other chocolate candies can also be used)
Coconut flakes
Mini marshmallows

Preparation method

Cut each banana down its inner center, leaving the peel on. Open each banana carefully and just wide enough to insert some filling. Stuff each banana with chocolate chips, coconut flakes, and mini marshmallows. Wrap each banana in tin foil, and place on the fire.

Let them cook for about 5 minutes. Allow banana to soften and chocolate chips to melt sufficiently. Test one of the bananas to see if it's cooked enough.

To serve, carefully open the packet. Remove some of the peel to form a large enough opening, and then eat the stuffed banana with a spoon directly in the packet.

NOTE: it is a good idea to use bananas that are at room temperature prior to cooking. If they are very cold, it will take longer.

Sweet & Spicy Popcorn

This popcorn recipe is easy and fun to make. It makes a great snack to munch on around the campfire.

Serves 4

Preparation time: 5 minutes

Cooking Time: 10-15 minutes

Cooking techniques: foil packets

Equipment: extra duty aluminum foil to make 4 large packets

Ingredients

1 cup popcorn kernels

1 cup vegetable oil

½ cup white granulated sugar

2 tablespoon cinnamon

Salt

Preparation method

Prepare 4 large aluminum foil sheet. Add a quarter of the corn kernel to each. Pour a quarter of the oil over the popcorn.

Fold the opposite corner of each packet together to form a dome and doing so leaving space for the kernels to pop. Seal all the edges well. Place the packets directly on the hot white coals Let the packet stand on the coals until the popcorn stops popping, shaking the packets a few time.

Whisk the sugar and cinnamon together in a small mixing bowl.

Remove the packets from the heat and open the top with caution, letting the steam out. Add some cinnamon sugar and a pinch of salt to each packet. Close the packets back again and give it a few shakes to combine the cinnamon sugar and popcorn well. Open and enjoy.

CONCLUSION

Eating in the great outdoors is one of the most wonderful experiences that both families and friends can share. Camping allows for activities we don't often get to have at home: hiking, canoeing, playing games by the campfire, but more so, camp cooking. Coming back to our "roots" and escaping from the buzz of the city life lets families get closer and individuals release the stress of normal life.

Hopefully, the recipes in this book have allowed for a delicious experience in the wilderness, one filled with family and friend time, and more importantly, meals to share with those you love.

ABOUT THE AUTHOR

Louise Davidson is an avid cook who likes simple flavors and easy-to-make meals. She lives in Tennessee with her husband, her three grown children, her two dogs, and the family's cat Whiskers. She loves the outdoor and has mastered the art of camp cooking on open fires and barbecue grills.

In colder months, she loves to whip up some slow cooker meals, and uses her favorite cooking tools in her kitchen, the cast iron pans, and Dutch oven. She also is very busy preparing Christmas treats for her extended family and friends. She gets busy baking for the holiday season sometimes as early as October. Her recipes are cherished by everyone who has tasted her foods and holiday treats.

Louise is a part-time writer of cookbooks, sharing her love of food, her experience, and her family's secret recipes with her readers.

She also loves to learn and share tips and tricks to make life.

Other books from Louise include:

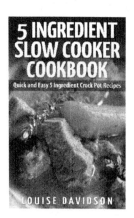

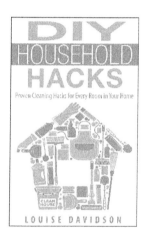

APPENDIX

Cooking Conversion Charts

1. Volumes

US Fluid Oz.	US	US Dry Oz.	Metric Liquid ml
¼ oz.	2 tsp.	1 oz.	10 ml.
½ oz.	1 tbsp.	2 oz.	15 ml.
1 oz.	2 tbsp.	3 oz.	30 ml.
2 oz.	¼ cup	3½ oz.	60 ml.
4 oz.	½ cup	4 oz.	125 ml.
6 oz.	¾ cup	6 oz.	175 ml.
8 oz.	1 cup	8 oz.	250 ml.

Tsp.= teaspoon - tbsp.= tablespoon – oz.= ounce – ml.= millimeter

CPSIA information can be obtained
at www.ICGtesting.com
Printed in the USA
LVOW04s2303120516

488026LV00035B/796/P